WORLDS APART

WORLDS APART

David Gribble

Libertarian Education

Libertarian Education is a small independent publishing collective, which for the past quarter of a century has been campaigning for the development of non-authoritarian intitiatives in education.

Also in this series:

For the latest information about Libertarian Education see http://www.libed.org.uk

Acknowledgements

Quotations from official documents and photographs are acknowledged in the text, but the words of current school students are anonymous, and it is to them that I must express my gratitude here. Their individual contributions make up almost half the book, but it is not only those whose work is included that I thank. Those whose comments were omitted because they were too similar to what others had already written, too extreme or too personal have also influenced the final shape of the book, and have helped to guarantee the accuracy of the impressions given.

Published by:
Libertarian Education, 84B Whitechapel High Street, London E1 7QX

ISBN 0-9551647-0-2 or 978-0-9551647-0-5

Copyright: David Gribble and Libertarian Education, 2006

Cover design by Jayne Clementson
Photograph byLuke Flegg

Printed and bound by:
Short Run Press, 25 Bittern Road, Sowton Industrial Estate, Exeter EX2 7LW
(Tel: 01392 211909)

CONTENTS

Introduction

There is a growing movement all over the world towards non-formal or democratic or free education. Representative examples are Butterflies, in Delhi, which offers street education to about 800 children, the Sudbury Schools in America and elsewhere which are growing in number, the Freinet movement in France and the Institute for Democratic Education in Israel. IDEC, the International Democratic Education Conference, is held each year in a different country, and attracts up to a thousand people.

In Great Britain these ideas are represented principally by Summerhill and Sands School.

The gulf between people who believe in this kind of education and people who prefer to see schools run on traditional lines is so great that they seem to live in separate universes. They accept some broadly similar aims, but their underlying philosophies are incompatible.

The following aims come from the prospectus of South Hunsley Comprehensive School:-

1. A Learning Community:

To be for all its members - pupils, teachers, non-teaching staff and parents - a true learning community, where the foundation of corporate life is the acceptance of a shared set of values which reflect the nature of learning itself.

2. Enjoyment and Participation:

To encourage enjoyment of learning and wide participation in all aspects of school life.

3. Equality of Worth:

To ensure that the learning of the child/student is the central concern of the school and to recognize and respond to the differences between individuals, whilst at all times according each equal worth, value, respect, care and consideration.

4. Access:

To recognize that all pupils have special educational needs and to meet these through a broad based and balanced curriculum which is accessible to all pupils regardless of abilities, gender or race.

In many democratic schools these words would be accepted too, but they would not have the same meaning. "A shared set of values," "a true learning community," "all aspects of school life" and "equal worth, value and respect," for instance, would all be differently interpreted. The purpose of this book is to illustrate these different interpretations, and what they actually mean to the lives of the students at the relevant schools.

It will also be necessary to tackle some of the prejudices which exist on either side of the divide. I have heard a head teacher from an informal school assert that in conventional education all that happens is that children learn information by heart and then reproduce it for exams. I have also heard a head of a grammar school announce that if, when he was a pupil, he had been allowed to discuss school rules he would have prolonged the discussion for the whole day, in order to avoid going to any lessons. Traditional educators who visit Summerhill are sometimes honestly surprised that none of the windows are broken. Advocates of alternative education are surprised in the same sort of way when they see children in conventional schools who are self-evidently happy.

Of course conventional schools differ from each other, just as free schools differ from each other, but on the scale between dictatorship and absolute freedom in education in Britain there is a wide gap between Sands and Summerhill and the rest. This becomes clear when the schools describe their own practice, and clearer still when the pupils describe their lives.

In the first section of this book I have, so far as possible, matched extracts from various state and public school prospectuses and websites with extracts from the published prospectuses and other documents of Summerhill and Sands. Where I have been unable to find passages that match significant statements from the other side of the divide, I have simply stated the opposite view in blunt terms; such passages are marked as editorial.

In the second and third sections I give accounts of pupils' school experiences in boarding schools and day schools. Before I approached anyone to ask for contributions, I wrote some descriptions of routine to show the sort of thing I was looking for. What appears here is mostly children's writing, sometimes a little edited to disguise its exact source, but even though everything has been checked and corrected by pupils from the relevant types of school, some of my original examples have survived almost unaltered. However, I wrote nothing unexpected or provocative; anything of that kind is authentic children's work.

I have not given any account of the large areas in which the aims of the two systems are indistinguishable. It must not be forgotten that even the strictest of authoritarian schools and even the most informal of free schools have this one fundamental aim in common – to do the best they can for the children who attend them. Conventional schools may lay more stress on exam results where the others think more of the personal growth of the child, but no one would quarrel with the suggested aims in the Warnock report, a survey of the educational provision for children with special needs, published in 1978:

> First to enlarge a child's knowledge, experience and imaginative understanding and thus his (or her) awareness of moral values and

capacity for enjoyment: and secondly, to enable him (or her) to enter the world after formal education is over as an active participant in society and a responsible contributor to it, capable of achieving as much independence as possible.

These should not be aims merely for children with special needs; as was correctly pointed out by South Hunsley Comprehensive School on an earlier page, they should be aims for all children. I hope this book will help to show which aspects of each type of school are most likely to contribute to the achievement of them.

The official view

Throughout this book the left-hand pages deal with traditional schools and the right-hand pages with democratic schools. The paragraphs on facing pages cover matching topics. It is best to read across the two pages, rather than reading right down each page in succession.

In this section the names of the schools are given after the quotations taken from their published documents. My own contributions are marked "Editor."

Basic philosophies

This is a school with a long tradition of providing a good education which, for at least a century and a half, has striven unequivocally to focus upon the development of the 'whole person.'

Uppingham School

We aim too to stimulate independent enquiry and intellectual curiosity, to enrich spiritual awareness, to match physical fitness with a love of the arts, and to promote individuality together with a sense of duty to friends and society.

Charterhouse School

Every pupil has the right to:
* Not to be teased or bullied in any shape or form
* Keep their own belongings safe, secure and untampered with
* Feel happy and secure as an individual, whatever their ability or needs
* A full and uninterrupted education
* Voice their own opinion politely and have a fair hearing
* Tell their personal problems to an adult.

Teesdale School

Basic philosophies

Summerhill was founded in 1921 by A.S. Neill, a Scottish teacher, writer and rebel. He wanted to create a community in which children could be free from adult authority.

Summerhill School

Summerhill does not aim to produce specific types of young people, with specific, assessed skills or knowledge, but aims to provide an environment in which children can define who they are and what they want to be.

Summerhill School

[The principles of the school] can be summarised as:
* The right to vote and participate in decision-making
* The right to choose one's own timetable
* The need to co-operate in caring for each other and looking after the building.

Sands School

The experience of holiness, an understanding of right and wrong, and respect for the worth of each human being; these things are the invisible glue holding our community together.

Rugby School

At the heart of Radley life is Chapel with daily weekday services for the whole school and families joining us for Sung Eucharist on Sundays.

Radley College

A few details

The current number on roll is approximately 1460 with a standard admission number of 232 pupils in Year 7, the year of intake.

Ashcombe School

I could tell you that the school has fourteen separate boarding houses, each with its own dining room. That it has 120 acres of land and wonderful facilities for theatre and games and art. That the whole site is networked for I.C.T. and that there are 1400 access points to the network for pupils and for staff. That it has an outstanding reputation in music. But what captivates the ordinary visitor to the school is the quality of the atmosphere.

Uppingham School

The experience of respect, trust and affection are the invisible glue holding our communities together.

Editor

There is no form of religious observance.

Editor

A few details

Currently there are seven staff and sixty-five students. It is our intention that Sands will always remain a small school.

Sands School

There are twelve acres of garden and woodland, with great places for off-road cycling, tree house building, climbing, walking, bonfires, camping, sunbathing, imaginative games. There is a swimming pool open during the summer, a tennis court, football field, basketball area, volleyball pitch, table tennis table and pool table.

. . . there are open areas including a Study Room (with 4 computers, open access web connection, and a growing library of CD Roms), the Art Room (with a photographic dark room), Pottery Room, the Music Room and the Woodwork Shop.

Summerhill School

Academic work

While embracing all of the key elements of recent educational change, the School is keen to preserve the best features of a traditional, broad, liberal education. No changes occur either in the content or style of teaching unless they can be justified on strictly educational grounds.

Diss High School

Each year, pupils have formal examinations. We also issue a full report and a progress review to parents and there is an annual Parents' Evening for each year group. Pupils are actively involved in this process. They review their progress and with the assistance of their tutors set personal targets for improvement which are then monitored. Tutors see pupils individually to discuss progress against the targets. This continuous process of review allows the school to monitor standards in general as well as the individual work of each pupil.

Ashcombe School

Of course all children have a full timetable of lessons from the moment they arrive, although sixth-formers may have some study periods. The school ensures that everyone follows a broad and balanced curriculum . . . From their very first days we ensure that all children make valuable use of their time in school.

Editor

Academic work

A new timetable is created every term to satisfy the choices of the children.

Summerhill School

[Our object is] . . . to allow children to be free from compulsory or imposed assessment, allowing them to develop their own goals and sense of achievement.

Summerhill School, General Policy Statement

Of course some children may come to Sands and do very little for weeks or months, or they may start courses and then abandon them. Some have very empty timetables or become obsessive about one or two individual activities to the exclusion of all others . . . Most children soon discover productive ways to spend their days. When a child becomes keen on one subject that soon leads on to other things. Timetables fill and days become busier.

Sands School

Homework is seen as of crucial importance to a child's academic success. It is given according to a published set of guidelines and noted in the pupil's diary which parents are encouraged to check regularly.

Diss High School

Physical Education is taught to all members of the school in the first two years. Pupils follow courses in a range of activities based on the National Curriculum. These include gymnastics, athletics, swimming and health-related fitness activities. Each pupil is required to achieve and acquire new skills as well as developing existing core skills. Regular national fitness tests are taken by the pupils.

Uppingham School

Those joining the CCF choose Army, Navy or RAF, and after completing a basic training course spend a year doing adventurous activities (similar to the Scout programme), followed by a compulsory holiday-time camp.

Charterhouse

The most important opportunity at our school is the opportunity to succeed. All lessons are compulsory.

Editor

This year 79% of our Year 11 pupils gained 5 or more A*-C grades at GCSE and almost half the pupils in Year 11 in this all-ability comprehensive school gained 9 grades A*-C.

Ashcombe School

Homework is necessary if children are to succeed in exams. It is given according to the discretion of the individual teachers in response to the needs of the children they are working with.

Editor

Physical Education is available to all members of the schools throughout their time. Pupils may choose to take part in a range of activities. Particularly popular at Sands are skateboarding, basketball, swimming and rock-climbing. At Summerhill off-road cycling can be added to the list. All activities are voluntary. There is no system of testing.

Editor

There are no Scouts and no CCF, Army, Navy or RAF. There are frequent opportunities for adventurous activities (similar to the Scout programme), and in the summer at Sands there is a voluntary term-time camp.

Editor

The most important freedom at Summerhill is the right to play. All lessons are optional.

Summerhill School

The school is a safe haven from society's increasing pressure on children to conform to adult expectations and standards. Despite continuous pressure from Government Inspectors we are proud not to be a factory for producing exam results.

Summerhill School

Most of the top independent schools, which are highly selective, have 100% of their candidates achieving five or more A* - C in GCSE. The average for comprehensive schools, which are by definition non-selective, and some of which are situated in deprived areas, is around 50%.

Editor

Destinations of leavers

Year 11:

Diss Sixth Form	58%
Further Education Colleges	25%
Employment without Training	10%
Modern Apprenticeship (Learning Gateway)	4%
Unemployed	1%
Not Known	2%

Sixth Form (Year 13):

Further Education	4%
Year Out	8%
Employment	31%
Higher Education	51%
Art Foundation	3%
Other	3%

Diss High School

At Sands School up to a quarter of the pupils have specific learning difficulties, and there are a number of refugees from conventional education who may need to postpone taking their GCSEs until Year 12. The proportion of Year 11 pupils gaining five or more A* - C grades, according to the published statistics, has varied from 11% to 67%.

Editor

What happens to students after Summerhill?

They go on to further study at college, or to do apprenticeships, or work, or travel. As an ex-Summerhillian states:
"If they (government inspectors) have any doubts about the place, the government should look at who we, Summerhillians, have become: we are artists, writers, professors, scientists, soldiers, administrators, theologians, bankers, musicians, carpenters, landscape architects, small business owners. We hold BAs, MAs and PhDs. We vote. We are precisely the 'useful people' their curricula is designed to produce! And we are happy and productive to boot."

Summerhill School

Consultation with pupils

School Council achievements

* Toilets improved.
* New bike stands purchased.
* Music system for the canteen and improved canteen atmosphere.
* Money raised for a number of charities.
* Trips organised to places like Chessington World of Adventure.
* Creation of Japanese garden.
* Helped solving of litter problem.
* New seating area created.

Notley High School

Discipline, rules and punishments

Discipline centres on the Housemaster, under the overall direction of the Second Master and ultimately the Headmaster.

Charterhouse School

Consultation with pupils

The weekly School Meeting is the hub of the Sands structure. It is the place where school policies are discussed and adjusted and where grievances are heard. It makes all the decisions that affect the school and takes on those responsibilities which are normally held by the head teacher.

Sands School

Discipline, rules and punishments

Discipline is entirely in the hands of the School Meetings.

Editor

The school has a number of strategies in place in order to encourage good attendance:

The Attendance Officer, Mr Anderson is responsible for maintaining attendance records.

First day response involves the school telephoning parents of absent children.

Attendance and punctuality figures are sent out to parents on a half-termly basis.

Pupils with poor attendance are encouraged to address this when setting personal targets.

Close liaison with police ensures that no pupil misses school unnecessarily.

The Knowsley Mayor's Award is achieved for 100% attendance.

A system of rewards involving stickers for achievement diaries, certificates and trips is used.

Halewood Community Comprehensive School

Selected Rules

Staff must always be addressed as 'Miss' or 'Sir'.

Pupils are expected to stand when an adult enters the classroom.

A 'keep right' rule operates throughout the school and pupils are expected to give way to adults.

Pupils must not wear coats in the classroom.

No chewing is allowed in lessons. Eating and drinking should be confined to break and lunchtimes.

Sands has one strategy in place in order to encourage good attendance – to remain a rational, happy place that children want to come to.

Summerhill adds to this a second strategy – it is a boarding school.

Editor

Contrasting Rules

[The rules below, made by children and staff together, differ so much from ordinary school rules that there are few which offer direct contrasts. The absence of certain rules is as significant as the presence of others.]

No eating in lab, drama room or meeting room.

Sands School

Pupils should only be out of class if they have written permission from a member of staff.

Pupils should be punctual for registration but on dry days must not enter the school buildings until the warning bell rings.

Cigarettes; felt-tip pens; aerosol cans;Tippex fluid; any electronic equipment including personal stereos; mobile phones; pagers; potentially dangerous items such as knives, matches and lighters are all prohibited – these items must not be brought to school. . . Pupils who disregard the rules will have items confiscated and held until parents collect them from school.

There must be no graffiti on exercise books.

All work should begin with Classwork/Homework, the date and title. A margin must be drawn on all pages and pages must be numbered.

Pontllanfraich School

On weekdays you can only go downtown from 5am - 9.30am and after 12 noon.

...

You are responsible for making and maintaining your own name-tag. You have to move your tag on the sign-out board before you leave the school premises and put it back when you return.

Summerhill School

You must not bring alcoholic drink or illegal drugs into school.

Sands School

Only Shack and over *[aged 13 +]* are allowed matches & lighters, but House kids *[aged 10 - 13]* can borrow them to light a fire in the woods.

Summerhill School

And more from Sands:-

No water fights in the building or above the wall in the garden.

If you break something you should replace or mend it yourself.

You may smoke, but only in the bottom half of the garden.

You may watch a video any time if you do not have a lesson.

And more from Summerhill:-

If you piss on the bog seat you have to wipe it off.

On your birthday you can go to the front of the queue.

Punishments include repetition of work, extra work and detention during breaks and lunchtime. We expect students to move about the school in an orderly manner, to treat the building with care, and to look after text books and materials provided. We will not tolerate disruptive behaviour in the classroom. Offenders will be withdrawn to work on their own. Highly disruptive or badly-behaved students may be placed in our Behavioural Support Unit or indeed excluded from school, as appropriate. We always try to be fair, reasonable and sympathetic to your child's side of the story before giving out punishment.

Kirkbalk School

School Uniform

Boys

Blazer	Black with school badge
Trousers	Plain charcoal grey (no jeans, chinos or other fashion trousers)
Shirt	Plain white
Tie	School tie
Shoes	Plain black or brown (no trainers or boots)

You will want to know what may happen if your child breaks any of these rules.

The first thing would be that another student or your child's tutor will speak to him or her about the problem. That may be enough. If those involved feel that your child understands the situation, is willing to reflect on it and to repair any damage caused then the affair is usually ended. For example, a broken window needs to be repaired by the person who broke it, and stolen property must be returned or replaced and an apology made. Common sense acts as our best guide, we try not to rely on precedents but to take each case on merit, allowing good sense to help us find a way through any conflict. It is generally felt that punishment prevents reflection and encourages the mistaken belief that retribution is an adequate response. Hence at Sands it is usually avoided, though it is often discussed. However, if children break very serious rules they may have to face a School Meeting. If the school feels that they cannot understand how to change their behaviour it will have no choice but to sanction them. If all else fails we may be forced to resort to expulsion, on the grounds that the child's views are incompatible with the school's principles.

Sands School Parents' Support Pack

No school uniform

You can wear whatever you like.

Editor

Girls

Jumper	V-necked bottle green (crew-neck pullovers are not allowed)
Blazer	Black with school badge
Trousers	Plain black tailored not fashion trousers
Skirt	Plain grey (knee length)
Shirt	Plain white school shirt
Tie	School tie
Socks	White or Black
Tights	Flesh or black
Jumper	V-necked bottle green (crew-neck pullovers, sweatshirts or cardigans are not allowed)
Shoes	Plain black or brown (no trainers, boots or fashion shoes) low heels.

Apron for C.D.T.

Topcoats should be plain and dark in colour.

If a student is not in the correct uniform, a written note from his/her parent should be produced asking the school for exemption for a specific time.

(PE Kit is described in detail, and then:-)

Jewellery / Make-up

Jewellery is not allowed except for a watch and for girls, a pair of ear studs/sleepers (not ear-rings). The wearing of make-up and nail varnish is not permitted in Years 7 - 10, Year 11 and Sixth form girls may wear discreet facial make-up.

The final decision regarding the acceptability of school uniform lies with the Headteacher.

Please contact the school if you are in doubt about a potential purchase.

St. Anselm's Catholic School

Parties and social life

Houses have their own Dinners for the different years at different times, which are black tie in some Houses. There are also the themed Bops. One particular theme, 'Street Names', caused a great deal of interest! Some of the Bops are for all the Lower Sixth or all the Upper Sixth only, some for both, and some Houses have similar events of their own.

On a more formal note, Upper Sixth Leavers have their own Leavers' Ball to look forward to at the end of their time with us. These are the more or less formal events which happen socially, but there are also many more. The Thring Centre, for instance, is the Sixth Form social centre, where Sixth Form pupils from all Houses can meet on Tuesday, Thursday, Friday, Saturday and Sunday evenings, and where there are theme evenings, such as 'Jungle', 'Valentines', 'Hawaiian' and 'Film Stars' evenings. There are Live Music nights where a few of the School bands play, Live D.J. evenings and there has even been the odd Karaoke night!

Uppingham School

The relationship between adults and children

All pupils are expected to . . . acknowledge the authority of all staff.

Kirkbalk School

Pupils have copies of the Home/School Contract in their achievement diaries which they and their parents are asked to sign and agree to support.

Halewood Community Comprehensive School

Parties and social life

During the winter and spring terms there is an elected Social Committee that organises games and activities in the afternoons and evening. These include capture and word games, board games, country dancing, storytelling, cafés, discussions, spontaneous acting, film trips . . .

There are two parties organised every term, halfway through and at the end. Lots of social events are used to raise money and the 'Lounge' is decorated with paper sculptures and wall paintings for great theme parties. Normally there is also a band, play or cabaret.

Summerhill School

The relationship between adults and children

The staff are trusted and their opinions are treated with respect.

Sands School

By their teenage years most children are hoping to find a little independence from home. If parents had too strong a voice at Sands, many children would probably choose not to take part in the executive work of the school.

Sands School

The core philosophy of the school is based on the common-sense view that in order to get the most out of an education you have to accept the decisions of experienced adults, that is to say teachers.

Editor

Personal development and responsibility

Academic achievement, personal responsibility and caring social attitudes are all underpinned by our concern to develop high self-esteem.

Ashcombe School

All classroom teachers aim to reward pupils with praise and supportive marking of work completed. Examples of good work are on display in classrooms and corridors. Pupils who complete successful residential courses, participate in sporting or musical events or who work hard for charities have achievement recognised in assemblies.

Halewood Community Comprehensive School

The school encourages good standards of behaviour by balancing a combination of REWARDS and SANCTIONS within a positive community atmosphere.

Halewood Community Comprehensive School

The core philosophy of the school is based on the common-sense view that in order to get the most out of an education you have to make decisions about what you want to do.

Sands School

Personal development and responsibility

Sands puts the well-being of the child before academic success. Unless children feel valued and respected, their work is of little importance to them.

Sands School

All classroom teachers have their individual styles, but it is a general practice to discuss the pupils' work with them. There is art displayed in the corridors, and staff decorate their own classrooms. Pupils who complete successful residential courses, participate in sporting or musical events or raise money for charities may well have a sense of achievement, but they may just have enjoyed themselves.

Editor

The schools encourage good standards of behaviour by a combination of RESPECT and TRUST within a positive community atmosphere.

Editor

We encourage individual expression within a framework of sensible discipline based on sound Christian values.

Charterhouse School

Traditionally, Charterhouse devotes one afternoon a week to service to the community both in the School and at large. The Combined Cadet Force and Scouts form part of this programme.

Charterhouse School

The school is maintained to a high standard by skilled professionals. Meals are planned with the advice of a dietician and prepared by experienced kitchen staff.

Editor

Senior boys are given responsibility as Prefects in helping to run the Social *[boarding house]*.

Radley College

As at most schools the central element of the life of Uppingham School is the classroom curriculum.

Uppingham School

Schools like Summerhill and Sands encourage individual expression within a framework of sensible behaviour based on the children's sound common sense.

Editor

Traditionally, the last quarter of an hour of every school day at Sands is devoted to maintenance, clearing up and other jobs. The school environment is genuinely the responsibility of the school community of staff and pupils. There is no compulsory community service outside the school.

Editor

Sands employs no domestic staff, so all the cooking, cleaning and washing up is done by the students and teachers. . . There is a weekly rota for washing up and everyone also has a Useful Work job to do in the last quarter of an hour of the school day.
Useful Work includes vacuuming, tidying up and generally keeping the school in a state of order. At intervals, when it is needed, more time is spent cleaning the school. At the beginning of each term, the whole building is given a day's intensive overhaul. Any decorating and minor repairs are also done by the students.

Sands School

Everyone shares in the responsibility for running the schools, from the youngest child to the oldest member of staff.

Editor

As in few other schools the central element of life in Summerhill and Sands is the people.

Editor

Boarding schools: a student's-eye view

Prospectuses and websites do not cover everything. Policies do not always achieve the intended results. Children, though, know how school life affects them personally.

In this section the left-hand pages describe experiences in a public school. Some of the authors are boys and some are girls; the youngest was twelve at the time of writing, and the oldest had just left school. A few alterations have been made to disguise the authors and their schools.

The right-hand page is about Summerhill and most of the text is by Summerhillians.

In both cases a few gaps have been filled in by taking information from other sources, but the whole text has been checked for accuracy by several pupils from appropriate schools.

Daily routine

The first bell goes at 7.00, and everyone has to be up and dressed by 7.30, which is breakfast time. Breakfast is compulsory and you have to sign in. The 6th form girls have their own rooms with en suite showers so they can easily shower and wash their hair. The lower school have dormitories, though, so that means there is quite a rush for the bathrooms and loos. Some boys stay in bed for as long as possible and then just jam their clothes on and hope to have time for a bit of a wash after breakfast is finished. A quick dab of deodorant is enough for some of them, though.

Breakfast is suppposed to be from 7.30 to 8.00, but some of the older students turn up later and manage to sit around until well after 8.00. It is compulsory to go to breakfast and you have to sign a register. In our house there is a large selection of cereals, cooked breakfast, yoghurt, tea and coffee. Everyone has a set place in the dining room for lunch, but you can sit somewhere different at breakfast if you want to. The house staff usually have breakfast on their own in their own part of the house.

Daily routine

The Beddies Officers go around and wake people up at eight o'clock in the morning. Beddies Officers are people who have been elected to enforce the bedtime and getting-up-in-the-morning rules. Sometimes a staff will run for election, but it's usually either Shack or Carriage kids *[aged 13+]*. There are three Beddies Officers for each day of the week and they split up in the morning to go to the different areas of the school. I'm usually up before this, outside in the summer or just chatting with friends in the dining room or somewhere in the winter. Some lazy sods sleep on for as long as possible, but the Beddies Officers go round again at 8.30 and anyone who is not out of bed gets fined. There is only one exception at the moment, which is George. The School Meeting has allowed him to sleep in until tea break at 11.10, because he says he works most in the evenings and if he has to get up early in the morning it just means he is walking around like a zombie for a couple of hours before doing anything useful. (School Meetings happen five days a week, on every weekday. All the staff and kids come and everything is decided there.)

Breakfast starts at 8.15. One of the teachers or a house-parent doles out cereal from the kitchen hatch in the corridor, and you can help yourself to tea and toast and marmalade in the dining room. They stop serving cereal at 8.45. The dining room has tables with blue tops and benches and as long as the weather's good it is bright and sunny. People just sit wherever they like and clear their stuff away when they have finished.

There are five lessons before lunch, plus Chapel three days a week. Everyone sings their heart out in Chapel and there is a reading by one of the prefects. It is really nice for the whole school to get together in the morning and it wakes you up having a good sing. When there isn't Chapel there are Tutor Periods.

There's a half-hour break at 11.00. You can get buns and cocoa in the boarding houses but they are revolting, so most people go to the buttery and buy sweets and sandwiches, etc., or have fruit and milk which goes down on your bill. It's a really sociable place.

Lunch is pretty formal. We eat in our houses, and in our house we have seven tables and each table has a 'guest' every day, either a prospective parent or a teacher. This can be pretty exhausting as all you want to do is chill out. Lunch is also compulsory with a register.

In the afternoon, lessons start at 2.00 and run till 6.00, with a twenty-minute break in the middle, except for Tuesday, Thursday and Saturday when there are games or activities. Games are compulsory, and if you miss them you get a detention. For boys it is rugby in the autumn, which is really hard, and not made easier by the autumn weather. In the spring we have hockey, football and cross-country. Everybody enjoys football, but not so much the other two. The summer is good, though, and we have swimming, athletics, cricket and tennis.

You sign up for activities at the beginning of the term, but nobody notices if you skip them so some people just go to the IT room or the library.

Lessons run all morning from 9.30 to lunchtime, but of course you don't have to go. One of the really amazing things is that none of the staff even try to persuade you to go. You just decide for yourself. Lots of the San kids *[aged 6 - 9]* just play outside nearly all the time, but just about everyone sees the point of learning stuff as they get older.

Class 3 and sign-up lessons finish at 1.10; Class 1 & 2 lessons finish at 12.20. Classes 1, 2 and 3 correspond roughly to Key Stages 1, 2 and 3, and at the beginning of each term anyone above Class 3 signs up for the timetabled lessons they want to go to.

Lunch is divided in two, because you can't get everyone in at a single sitting, and younger kids finish lessons earlier.

The next lot of lessons starts at 4.00, so everyone has the afternoon free to do whatever they like. People go down into town, or organise games, or climb trees or mend bicycles or just sit and talk. I used to have a camp where I would go just about every day with my two special friends and we would creep in underground and light a fire and toast marshmallows or whatever. In the summer most people spend ages in the pool.

Prep is from 7.00 until 9.00. You are supposed to do this in your own room and not talk but I spend most of my time in Annabel's room playing Monopoly. On Fridays there is sometimes a talk by someone supposedly interesting, which your houseparents are bound to want you to go to, or a concert or a film or a play. I always go to the plays and concerts, but otherwise but I prefer to stick around and talk to my friends.

Tea is at 6.30 and is less formal than lunch because there are no guests. There is supposed to be a mixing of age-groups. The house captain reads out the notices for the next day, and Matron takes another register. It is inclined to be a bit sparse – ham and salad, or eggs and bacon, or cauliflower cheese.

After prep you can go out of the house until your bedtime, but you have to sign out. You always have to sign out, even in the daytime, if you are going to do anything except for games and lessons.

Boys are only allowed in the girls' houses on Monday, Wednesday and Friday after prep and on Saturday after games at 4.00 and then from 9.00 until 10.20. They are not allowed upstairs, and we have restricted areas for them. In our house we have a large common room with a TV and a pool table, but it's usually dominated by the sixth form, so the lower school doesn't get much of a look in.

Lessons sometimes go into the evening. There are discussions and talks in the café and there are always various staff around to do things with if you want to.

Supper is at 5.20 for everybody, and ends at 6.15. It's not like my last school, where the staff sat at the ends of the tables and told everyone not to talk too loudly, but everyone sits together, just mixed up – although you tend to sit with your friends, and that sometimes means the staff get into a kind of bunch.

The food is OK and there is always a choice, particularly at lunch. There's always a choice of vegetarian or non-vegetarian with rice and noodles, because there are lots of Asian kids, and there's lots of fruit. The kitchen staff are called the Queens of Custard.

The little kids aren't allowed out of the school grounds on their own, and there are all sorts of laws to govern who is allowed to do what. However old you are you have to be back by 10.00, but if you are mad enough you are allowed to get up and go out as early as five o'clock in the morning.

There are discos three evenings a week, although they aren't called discos, they're called grams, which only goes to show how long they have been going on. Even my parents didn't have gramophones. It's all organised by the gram committee, who play the music and work the lights and everything. The staff often complain that it is all too loud and I agree.

After prayers it's time for the lower school to get ready for bed, but for the rest of us it's the first decent stretch of free time in the day. It's lights out at 9.00 for the Year Sixes, and it gets later as you get older, until the Upper Sixth when it is up to you. We Year Sixes are supposed to be on our beds reading quietly for twenty minutes before lights out, but no one is. Most people are on their mobile phones or listening to music. It's the house prefects who have to make sure that everyone gets to bed on time, and the housemaster or -mistress comes round and checks up.

Lights out is meant to mean no talking, but we normally stay awake for at least two hours. Some people bring in a laptop and a DVD for us to watch, or people text their friends. I sometimes read by torchlight. If you are caught the penalties are severe, but most feel it is worth the risk. I remember once being caught talking at about midnight in exam week, so I had to get up at 6.30 to revise for an hour. We sometimes go dorm-raiding, which is quite fun, but by Year Eight people are normally bored with it.

Anyone who is actually up after lights out gets to have to go to bed early or gated or whatever, depending on what time it was. The house is alarmed, so if you leave your corridor the intruder alarm goes off and everyone has to stand outside their rooms and be counted by the house staff.

The grams aren't the only things that go on in the evenings. People play outside games like Kick the Can or British Bulldog, or they sit in the houseparents' rooms or the staff room and just talk, or go down the town to the Indian or the Chinese takeaways or the chip shop, or go to the cinema or stay in and watch TV or play computer games. (One of the Indian takeaways will actually deliver to the door.) Nobody much watches TV unless there is some special programme, because there is always so much else going on. The only time I watch much TV is at home in the holidays.

Bedtimes are decided by the Meeting and supervised by the Beddies Officers. Bedtime for the San kids *[6 - 9]* is 8.00 to 9.00, but at the other extreme Carriage kids *[14+]* have just voted for an 11.30 bedtime. From lights out, when the Beddies Officers actually turn the lights out, until wake-up is called silence hour, and you can get fined if you make too much noise or don't do what the Beddies Officers tell you. It doesn't always work, though, and people who are trying to get to sleep have to threaten to fetch the Beddies Officers, and even then it may not work until they have had to come back two or three times. The last part of the evening is just an exciting time, and people don't want it to end. New kids are always the worst. After you have been here a while you get used to it.

Weekly routine

There are no exeats during the term but depending on the urgency of the requests occasionally they allow you to go. Weekends have good bits and bad bits. On Saturday afternoon there is always sport, but in the evening there is usually a film or a concert or a play or something. It's Sunday afternoon that can get a bit dire, after you've written a letter home and gone to Chapel and sat around and chatted for a while. You have to sign in or answer a roll-call four times a day even at the weekend, so you don't have time to go anywhere, and you aren't allowed to visit the day people's homes. There are good things sometimes, like indoor cricket, which is against the rules because windows sometimes get broken, or sneaking off somewhere for a fag, but generally you just hang around waiting for supper time. People who like role-playing games get really into them, and some people play chess, too, but cards aren't allowed because we might be gambling.

Every Tuesday afternoon the Fifth- and Sixth-Formers have to dress up as soldiers and go off and do CCF training. The good thing about that is that occasionally you get a field day when you have a whole day off school and go and play at battles with blank ammunition in some wild part of the country somewhere.

There is an alternative, which is Voluntary Service, which is compulsory. You work with young children or disabled people and that sort of thing.

Weekly routine

On Friday afternoon we get poc *[-ket money]*. If you've been fined for anything during the week it gets deducted. And almost everybody goes down to the town on Saturday morning to spend it, or at least to spend some of it.

On Saturdays there is brunch, which is an old-fashioned English breakfast, which almost everyone loves.

The café has been totally refurbished and even has a carpet now, and some beanbags. There's a TV and a computer, and it's open all day for things like drama, cooking, discussions, chess and quiet games, massage and just hanging out. It's called the Jazz Café but it doesn't sell coffee and usually doesn't play jazz. There was a Korean night last term when they cooked Korean food for anyone who signed up.

There's a good deal of religion. Religious Studies, which we have twice a week, can be very interesting because we do other religions besides Christianity and we make comparisons, and besides all that it's a very easy GCSE. But that's only the beginning. There's morning chapel most days and prayers in the boarding houses every evening, when you all get together in the dining room and the housemaster or housemistress reads a few prayers and you all say "Our Father." And in most houses there is grace before lunch, and on Sundays morning chapel is compulsory, but evening chapel is voluntary. There's communion early in the morning, too, for people who have been confirmed, and there is a good deal of pressure to get confirmed, even if your parents never got you christened. I quite like Chapel because I enjoy singing hymns and you get a bit of time to yourself when the prayers are going on. For some people it's really important, but it can be funny when people sing wrong words to the hymns.

Hardly anyone does anything practical about religion, like going to church or saying prayers or anything, but there are some people who do. There are occasionally people on the staff who are into weird New Age stuff. It all makes for good discussions.

Domestic arrangements

The dormitories for lower school aren't as bad as they used to be. There's usually only about six to a room, for one thing, and everyone has a chest of drawers and a desk and a wardrobe. The beds are fairly comfortable, as long as you bring a duvet from home. Otherwise the house only gives you sheets and blankets. The Sixth Form have their own bedsitters which they can furnish as they like, as long as they don't put sexy posters on the walls. It may be different in the girls' houses, I don't know. Everything has to be kept spotlessly tidy or the domestic staff complain and get you tortured.

The housemasters or housemistresses are very important figures, but I hate mine. Mrs. G. is just like David Brent in 'The Office' and Mr. G. is a bully. They both teach, too, so they never really have time to talk. There are lots of the staff I really like, though, and most houses have resident pets, which can keep you company when you are feeling low.

Domestic arrangements

People live in separate buildings according to age. In the San *[for ages 6 - 9]* boys and girls sleep in separate dormitories but with a connecting door, but after that the sexes get divided. Until you are a Carriage kid you share a room with three or four others. The floor is vinyl or carpet, and you have a bed and a cupboard which is just about big enough to keep your clothes and a few books or toys. Most people brighten the place up with a few posters and things. The House boys *[11 - 13]* are inclined to be disgustingly untidy and dirty, but they have to obey three rules: 1) they can't leave a mess for someone else to pick up; 2) they have to pay for any damage; 3) the Meeting can fine them if they are so messy it affects someone else's freedom to enjoy their environment. There is a health and safety committee that checks on the conditions of rooms and the equipment in them. They report back to the Meeting on people who are causing trouble. There is also a special rooms ombudsman who can be called in to arbitrate on issues to do with tidiness and hygiene. That's when people sometimes get the Minimum Stuff Fine *[see below]*.
Carriage kids usually have hi-fis and posters and bedspreads used as hangings.

Houseparents are not like real parents. They will help you if you really need it but most of the time they just leave you alone to do whatever you want. It's no good going to Carmel if you are a San kid and complaining about what someone else has done or said. You have to go to an ombudsman or bring it up at the Meeting. And if you think your houseparents are being unfair then you can bring them up at the Meeting and they may get a fine, just like anyone else.

Uniform is not too bad, and I am pleased we have it because on home clothes day people often get teased if their clothes aren't really expensive. In the evenings when we wear home clothes no one gets teased, though, because most of the boarders are quite close to each other and don't want to hurt each other.

In the winter the girls wear long black skirts, white shirts, grey jumpers and long black coats with a house scarf, and in the summer short grey skirts, white shirts and a blazer. The staff are strict about skirt lengths and so on, but at the discos they just wear hot pants and bras, which is great.

Clothes are terribly important when you live in a dormitory. If you wear anything markedly different to anyone else, like pants instead of boxer shorts, for instance, you look a real idiot. You have to wear the school uniform all day except during sport, but after the end of lessons and after lunch on Sundays you can change into home clothes, as long as it doesn't include baseball caps for the boys or strappy tops for the girls or anything like that. They say that strappy tops would provoke the male teachers.

You put your own dirty laundry in your laundry bag and make your own laundry list. There's no one to do it for you.

There are a few days [i.e. *not boarders*], but they have to be in school by half past eight and they don't leave until supper time, so you hardly notice the difference. Theoretically they are freer once they get home, but they can't have their friends round and there is always so much prep that more or less all they can do is go home, do their prep and go to bed. They have more free time at the weekends, though, unless they have to come in for school matches or orchestra or whatever.

You can wear whatever you like. New kids love it because they can dye their hair blue and get their ears pierced. Some kids, mainly boys, go around dirty all the time from climbing trees or building camps or hanging around a bonfire. If you get too disgusting, though, your houseparent will get onto you. Some people are fashion-conscious and can afford expensive trainers, but I just dress for comfort.

Houseparents do the laundry for everyone except Carriage kids. Some Shack kids want to be allowed to do their own laundry too, because there is an evil sock-eating monster, but they aren't allowed to.

If you are a day kid you can feel left out of things. Some of the younger ones hide at the end of the day so that their parents won't find them when they come to pick them up, and Beth likes her animals too much to leave them. Most of the day kids would really like to be boarders.

Facilities

There's a full-size Olympic swimming pool which we use for PE once a week, but otherwise it's kept for the really serious swimmers who haul themselves up and down the lanes over and over again, and usually win when there is a match against anyone else.

The school theatre is fantastic, with raked seating and a really professional lighting board and a huge space for scenery and everything. They do really good plays there, but you don't get a chance of a part unless you are pretty special. Most of the time you just do drama in drama lessons, or in house plays, which usually happen in the dining room. They're good fun too, though.

The choir and the orchestra are absolutely brilliant. There are eight people in our house in the choir and three in the orchestra, because we're not a particularly musical lot, but we make up for it in sports.

The art room seems to have just about everything – poster paints, oil paints, watercolours, lino-printing stuff, screen-printing, pottery wheels, sculpture, welding – but you don't get to do much of all that in the actual lessons, because you can't have twenty-five people all doing etching at the same time because there just isn't enough stuff. The best thing to do is to go in the evenings and at the weekends, when you can work on whatever you like.

Facilities

We've got a swimming pool that is just used for swimming in, not for training, although you can go to swimming lessons if you want to. There are rules about supervision and stuff, but on the whole you can just go and swim whenever you want to.

We've got a theatre with a stage and lights, but the people who want to act have to share it with the rock band who practise in there. Sometimes a member of staff organises a play, but usually we just do our own.

There are quite a lot of good musicians, considering how small the school is, but it isn't enough to make an orchestra. There are always rock bands, though, and at the moment there is a choir that performs at the EOT *[End of Term party]*.

The art room and the woodwork room are two of the spaces that are kept locked when there isn't a staff there. It's just too tempting to go in and splash paint around, or to borrow the woodwork tools to help build your camp or something and then forget to take them back.

Punishments

Given by staff

Writing sides. If you have done something inappropriate you have to write about why you have done it and why it is inappropriate.

Confiscation. Inappropriate items get confiscated.

Being gated, which means you have to stay in your house all evening. You get a job to do, like polishing trophies or sanding desks. You get gated for missing games or meals or a roll-call. If you come back to your house after your set time you get gated and probably detention as well. I've been gated twice, once for coming in twenty minutes late and once for not making my bed.

Detention happens at half past six on a Saturday morning. You have to write an essay of little relevance to anything for two hours.

Internal rustication. That means you can't leave the house for any reason at all except to go to lessons. You can't go to games, and you have to come back and stay in your room in every break time.

Being sent to the headmaster - usually for stealing or bullying.

Suspension. That means being sent home for a while. A friend of mine was caught in her boyfriend's room, not doing anything, but she had been banned from his house and she was suspended for 48 hours.

Expulsion. Sex, drugs or large amounts of spirits and you get expelled, no questions asked.

Punishments

Given by the School Meeting

Strong reminder.

Strong warning, which is stronger than a strong reminder.

Fines. Sometimes this means having to pay a fine, like it does in ordinary law, and sometimes it means any kind of punishment or losing a privilege.

SJF, MJF and LJF. These stand for Small, Medium or Large Job Fines, which mean cleaning stuff or working in the garden.

TBF - Tea Biscuit Fine, no biscuits at tea.

Share-a-Cake Fine. This is for when two people have a dispute. They have to talk about it with an ombudsman while they share a cake.

BOLQ - Back of the Lunch Queue.

BOAQ - Back of All Queues.

MSF - Minimum Stuff Fine, which is usually just for leaving your room in a mess. It means you aren't allowed to have anything except a change of clothes, a bit of soap, a towel and a bit of toothpaste on a toothbrush.

Bullies List. You get your name on a Bullies List.

Screen Ban. No TV or computer games.

Wheels Ban. No cycling or skateboarding.

You can also get fined proportions of poc *[-ket money]* so you may hear Beddies Officers saying, 'You've got 10%.'

Punishments given by prefects

havinɡ to ɡo to bed early

havinɡ to ɡet up early

extra chores

fines

not being allowed to watch TV

Smoking, alcohol, drugs and sex

There have been two innovations in the last few years that I really approve of. One is the Sixth Form bar, where you can buy beer and wine in the evenings, and the other is girls in the school.

GIRLS!!! We've only had girls in the school for about five years, and now there are almost as many girls as boys. They don't seem to affect me too much, mainly because I was previously at a mixed school, but there are occasions when certain young fillies make you look twice!

There's a tradition that all the new girls have to be debagged, which means pulling down their trousers or lifting their skirts, and they get marked out of ten.

Boys and girls date. If a boy wants to kiss a girl he asks to 'walk her back' at the end of the evening.

Smoking, alcohol, drugs and sex

After the San there are separate dormitories for boys and girls, but everyone mixes together all the time and people swim naked in the pool and we've all known each other for such ages that sex just doesn't come into it. You can sit on a boy's lap without thinking twice. There's a craze for massage at the moment, and you can get anyone to massage you, boy or girl. Touching people is just natural, it isn't sexy unless you mean it to be.

Sometimes pairs write themselves up on the board opposite the kitchen, and you see them walking around holding hands and kissing in the lunch queue. There aren't usually many serious pairs, though – there's only one at the moment.

You are not allowed to hold hands in the street or kiss in public. This means there are a lot of couples sneaking around and hiding. Sex does happen but normally only when relationships are really serious. The girls are allowed into the boys' rooms and you can lock the door from the outside. If you are caught having sex you are expelled. Even if you are caught 'with no feet on the ground' you are in big trouble.

Ours is one of the few schools to run urine sample tests for drugs. They take place once every blue moon. Each time a group of students is chosen at random. One term two people I really liked got expelled for testing positive.

(BUT compare this with the following entry.)

As far as I know there is no problem with drugs at my school, not even weed. There is a lot of alcohol around, though. You are allowed to buy three glasses of wine or two beers when the school bar is open, which is for a couple of hours each on Wednesdays, Saturdays and Sundays. There are teachers working behind the bar. Normally people have a drink in the house before they go there, but if you get caught with spirits in your room you get sent home, and if you are caught with wine you get gated. At the official school parties you are allowed four glasses of wine, but everyone is breathalysed before they are allowed in.

You are allowed limited alcohol at the house dinners, too. Each house has one dinner a term, and we organise them ourselves, the food and the music and everything. Everyone can invite one guest.

Smoking happens, but there is no peer pressure to do it. If you get caught once you are fined £5 and gated for one night, and if you are caught again it is £10 and gated for two nights and so on.

Zoe talks to us Carriage kids occasionally about what the law says about having sex before you are sixteen and about contraception, so we know how things are.

There is an absolute ban on drugs and alcohol. If you bring either into the school you get sent home.

Smoking is allowed, although the Meeting is always trying to think of ways of limiting it. At the moment you are only allowed to smoke away from the buildings, and you can't smoke if there are any young kids around.

Hierarchies and rebels

Although personal fagging is long gone, there is still a sort of class structure. Juniors are still expected to show their respect and admiration for brilliant people like me. But you don't lose face by speaking to people younger than you. Juniors are sometimes even allowed to come into Seniors' studies.

Some of the staff call us by our first names but we all call them Sir or Mrs. Macintosh or whatever. It would make authority impossible if we were allowed to called them Brian and Nancy. It makes me laugh even to think of it.

It is clear to me that the boys in my house, and others, as well as the most recent batch of leavers, would like to see the houses run as they were five years ago. Not because of the housemasters, but because of the interaction with the younger boys. Of course there should be no bullying of any kind in a school of the class and calibre of ours, but I look at certain juniors who have been cheeky too many times, and I wish . . .
Something has changed, and I just hope it doesn't change any more.

[BUT a younger contributor wrote this.]

There is some bullying, but usually things settle down soon enough, and having separate houses also helps to prevent bullying. In Year Seven I felt slightly bullied but my housemaster talked to everyone involved and now we are all good friends. Generally the older kids look after the younger ones as they feel they have a responsibility. Lots of us have friends in the Sixth Form, for example.

Hierarchies and rebels

Everyone calls everyone else by their first names or their nicknames. No one ever gets called Miss or Sir.

Rebels come in two forms – there are accepted rebels and non-accepted rebels. The accepted rebels even have prefects as friends and often get on particularly well with the staff. They rebel by having secret love affairs and selling cannabis and going out at night and never getting caught. The unaccepted rebels are usually rather dim and unpopular and just try to get themselves noticed by disrupting lessons and picking on people and sometimes even stealing things. The prefects and the staff are just as pissed off with them as everyone else is.

Summing up

Everyone here has had to pass the entrance exam, so they're all pretty bright. That means that if you're only expected to get Bs and Cs in your GCSEs like me, you feel you're useless, and letting your parents down. It's definitely not cool to be seen to be working too hard, though. You are supposed to do well, but without really trying.

We are really lucky to be at a school like this with excellent facilities and some great teachers. If there's anything you really want to get good at, like cricket or music or golf or drama or anything at all, you get first class tuition and masses of opportunity and encouragement.

The only way not to enjoy yourself here is by not making good use of the opportunities available. Most people like that leave after a couple of months, but there are very few of them. As long as people have a sense of purpose and have their priorities they will do well. As long as there is something you like, even if it is only clarinet lessons or doing house plays, you can always look forward to that and really do well in it.

There are hardly any rebels at Summerhill because there is nothing to rebel against except the School Meeting, and in my opinion the School Meeting is totally sensible. There are people who pinch things, or ride other people's bikes, or break various rules, but they aren't exactly rebels, they're just getting rid of all the stuff that has been done to them before. But there are sometimes people who just drop out of community life and don't ever go to any lessons, and then that comes up in a Career Chat. Some of them leave early to go and take exams at schools where they will get their arses kicked if they don't work.

Summing up

There's no entrance exam, there's just an interview with Zoe. You can't come if you are older than eleven, though. Older people who come from strict schools don't know how to use the freedom. You can take exams whenever you are ready to, but some people leave with no exam passes and go on to be very happy and successful.

The only way not to enjoy yourself here is by making yourself totally unpopular. And that's pretty difficult, because we're fairly tolerant on the whole, and if you do piss people off you get told about it and you learn.

It's sometimes tough, particularly in the lower school, but at the end of it you come out as someone with real qualities, who stands out as an interesting kind of person and gets automatic respect. And what's more most people at this school are very happy and make life-long friends.

Thank God I'm at Summerhill (even though I don't believe in him). I'm just able to be myself, and I've learnt to allow other people to be themselves too. I'm going to get the GCSEs I need without too much hassle, and I know what I want to do next, which is to get the right A-Levels to get into Art College. I've enjoyed my childhood, and I'm going to enjoy being grown-up too. Nothing's going to stop me.

Photographs

English lesson: Sands School

Uniforms: Plymstock School

PLYMOUTH EVENING HERALD

SANDS SCHOOL

No uniforms: Sands School

A small part of Dulwich College

DAVID GRIBBLE

Break time: football: Ivybridge Community College

PLYMOUTH EVENING HERALD

ZOE READHEAD

Most of Summerhill School

SANDS SCHOOL

Break time: grandmother's footsteps: Sands School

School Chapel: Harrow School   XIN PANG

Military training: Harrow School   XIN PANG

ZOE READHEAD

School Meeting: Summerhill School

ZOE READHEAD

Camp fire and tree house: Summerhill School

71

From the back of the class: Harrow School

XIN PANG

Media studies: South Dartmoor Community College

LUKE FLEGG

SANDS SCHOOL

From the back of the class: Sands School

ZOE READHEAD

English as a foreign language: Summerhill School

Football fields: Devonport High School for Boys

Indoor games: Hele's School

SANDS SCHOOL

Tennis court: Sands School

ZOE READHEAD

Indoor games: Summerhill School

75

Bill:Harrow School

Music: St. Dunstan's Abbey School

SANDS SCHOOL

Register: Sands School

Music: Sands School

SANDS SCHOOL

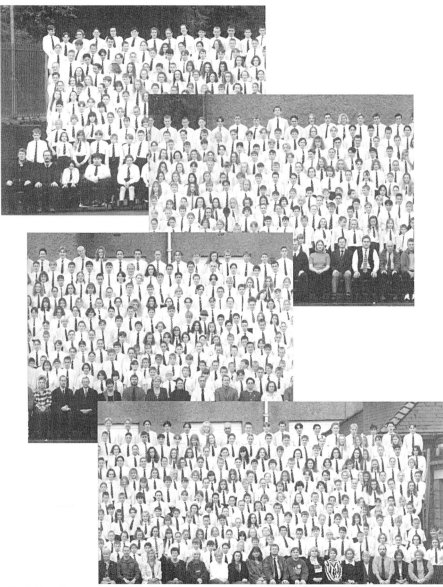

Newbridge Comprehensive School

SANDS SCHOOL

Sands School

ZOE READHEAD

Summerhill School

Post-GCSE shirt-signing: South Dartmoor Community College

LUKE FLEGG

Day schools: a student's eye view

Some of the more routine passages from the following student's eye accounts were actually written as examples to show students what was wanted, but were accepted without question as accurate. The rest are authentic students' work. All of them have been checked for accuracy, and where necessary corrected or re-written by members of appropriate schools. There are some collations of material written by several different students, and there are also paragraphs written in deliberate imitation of comments made by students from the other side of the fence, with a few relevant words altered.

The comprehensive school described on the left-hand pages is a composite, and fairly middle-of-the-road. There is no rioting and there are no authoritarian excesses. The school on the right-hand pages is Sands.

The start of the day

The bus drops us off in the big bus-park at the side of the school. It's a smart new building with regular rows of windows on three floors, and the main entrance is through big double doors that swing back and catch you if you don't watch out. Inside there are wide corridors going off in three different directions, all looking exactly the same. The walls are greeny white, and there are always big displays of art on the pinboards.

The first thing you do when you get inside is to go to your tutor room and wait until the teacher arrives and does the register.

The classrooms are all fitted out with about thirty desks in neat rows but for registration Mr. W. allows us to sit about where we like. After the register we have a bit more time to chat while he deals with one or two individual queries or problems.

When the register is done we all have to line up by the door and then he sends us off and we have to walk down the corridor in single file. Mr. W. sometimes gets a bit stressed because that's when all the other teachers can see how well he manages his group.

The start of the day

Most people get dropped off outside the front gate to the school, which is on the main street of Ashburton, but the minibuses drive right in. It's a rather dilapidated old building which was once just a big family house, and the main entrance is through an ordinary sort of family house front door. Inside there's a dark hallway with a floor made of coloured tiles. It opens out into a stairwell at the far end, where the daylight shines in. The walls are covered with artwork and pinboards with every kind of notice on them – school lists, newsletters, things for sale, whatever anyone wants to put up.

The first thing I usually do is go to the kitchen to make myself a mug of coffee to take to my first lesson, but there are always rather too many people in there and sometimes it isn't worth the hassle. A few people go down the garden where you are allowed to smoke and maybe smoke a quick rollie or share a straight between two or three people. *[This was written before the latest move to ban smoking, described page 105.]*

The register is kept in the office where Vicky just checks who's not in school by looking and asking round.

If it's sunny some people sit on the terrace, or you can go to a classroom to try to catch one of the teachers to ask about something, or just to sit around and chat. Whatever the weather is like the skateboarders will probably get started, even if it's only for a few minutes. And a few people will probably be playing in the music room.

When we get to the hall we have to sit down on the floor. Mr. V. stands on the stage at the front and shouts at anyone who talks or pushes or tries to eat a sweet or doesn't sit properly. Sometimes he has to send people out, and they have to stand in the corridor outside and go to see the head later on. The floor is polished wood, and it is not exactly comfortable.

When all the pupils are sitting on the floor then the staff come in and sit on chairs on the stage, and last of all comes Mr. G. He says a few prayers and talks about something in the news or tells us an uplifting moral story, or else he gives us a lecture about school uniform or smoking on the buses or running in the corridors or something. And then the other staff take it in turns to make announcements about sports fixtures and timetable changes and outings.

And then the staff go out and we all stand up, one row after another, and go back to our tutor groups to pick up our bags and set off to our first lessons.

Lessons are supposed to start at half past nine but they hardly ever do because assembly goes on for too long or the staff stay behind to discuss something.

We don't have any assembly.

There are notices by the front door about what is actually happening today, and there are more notices in the hall about all kinds of different things, like trips and so on, so it's a good idea to have a look at all that every once in a while, or you may miss out on something.

And then when it's getting towards a quarter to ten people begin to move off and you realise it's time for lessons to start.

Lessons start at 9.45. A few years ago they were supposed to start at half past nine, but everyone was always late. Now people come on time.

Buildings, facilities and organisation

The building was designed as a school, of course, so nearly all the classrooms are the same, more or less square with windows on to the outside world on one side and windows into the corridor on the other. At the end where the teacher's table is there is a whiteboard that goes all along the wall, and at the other end there is a huge pinboard which most teachers use to display posters, to give the room some character. In the middle there are these thirty desks, in five rows of six, with little grey plastic chairs with metal legs. It's only the labs and the art and craft rooms that are any different.

Outside there is a big tarmac playground, a few temporary classrooms that have been there for ever, a bit of grass and about six trees.

The person who runs the whole place is the headmaster. He has his deputies and the heads of year and the heads of departments, and then there are the other teachers, and then there's us. We're the raw material they work on, or, to put it another way, they're the people who have to make something out of us. They make all the everyday decisions and the headmaster makes the big ones. We only decide small things for ourselves, like where to sit in the classroom, which some teachers let us decide, or who we want for friends and what we are going to do in break.

Buildings, facilities and organisation

The building was designed as a house so it's comfy and doesn't feel sterile. All the rooms are different and have been changed a lot by the students and teachers. There are sofas and armchairs in some of them (even in the science room), so you can sit comfortably for a discussion or when you want to watch a video. The rooms are generally messy with tables in clusters in the middle of the room. There are carpets on the floor almost everywhere, so it's comfortable even if you want to sit on the floor. There are lots of pictures and posters of all sorts of things (anything anyone wants to put up) and books and bits of paper everywhere.

There is a *huge* garden and some smaller buildings for things like art and woodwork and an independent pre-fab building for a lab. Also there is a summerhouse further down the garden where some people smoke or just hang out.

The organisation that runs the whole place is the School Meeting. That's all the children and all the staff, with one vote each if it comes to voting. There's an administrator instead of a head, and that person has to do whatever the School Meeting decides, and so do the teachers. Well, so do we all, but it's all of us together who decide. That's big decisions. Little ones you make for yourself, like who you hang around with and what lessons you want to go to.

Joanna cooks the school lunch in the morning and is the secretary in the afternoon. She is the true ruler of this place of chaos – the Goddess of Food and Organisation.

There is a student council, and the head is always there. We discuss arrangements for parties and Red Nose Day, and the colour schemes in the classrooms and sometimes we get as far as commenting on school dinners, but otherwise nothing we say seems to have much effect. We're never allowed to make any decisions, only recommendations, and as it actually works out we're not even allowed to make any criticisms. Even if they're disguised as suggestions they get slapped down. The head seems to take everything personally, which means that nothing changes.

The curriculum is the same for everybody. The only way you can get out of anything is by going to college to do a course in brick-laying or something. Most people do ten or eleven GCSEs, so you get the opportunity to achieve very highly. Even the people who are only going to get Fs or Gs still have to try for at least eight or nine exams, including GNVQs, etc. If you gave them the choice of that or doing nothing they'd just skive off school and cause trouble.

If you don't like one teacher or one subject it's fairly easy to bunk off after registration and take refuge in the lavatories. There's a fence all round the grounds, but the gates are left open during the daytime and anyway you can get through the fence behind the boiler-house, but you'll probably get suspended if you get caught. For some people, though, that's more like a reward than a punishment.

We've got a huge playing field and a gym and labs for all three sciences and a home economics room with all different kinds of cooker and a woodwork shop and a metalwork shop and an art room with all kinds of painting and drawing equipment and music rooms with free lessons in playing an instrument. The facilities are always being improved and they've just built a recording studio and soundproof practice rooms.

The School Meeting discusses and decides about anything and everything. We appoint the staff, we get the timetable changed, we invent new schemes for the clearing up at the end of school, we deal with discipline problems, we plan school camps, we make rules for special situations like when there was a craze for waterfights last summer and we admit new pupils. We decide everything the head would normally decide, only it's often the administrator and the other teachers who have to make sure it is put into practice. It's our school and we are always trying to make it better, so it changes all the time.

The timetable is the same for everybody, but you don't have to do a subject if you don't want to. Most people do six or seven GCSEs, but some people only do one or two, and very occasionally there is someone, usually a pretty bright and determined person, who doesn't do any. The people who are going to have difficulty are able to use their time to concentrate on the subjects that interest them.

If you don't like one teacher or one subject you can just not go, and practise basketball or go across the road to the shop and get something to eat or play a computer game or go down the garden to where the smokers are and join in the conversation.

We've got a big garden and an astroturf court and one lab for all three sciences and a kitchen where we can help cook lunch if we want to and a woodwork room and an art room where you can do pottery and welding as well as painting and drawing and a music room where the band plays. If you want lessons on an instrument then you have to pay extra.

In break time everyone has to go out into the playground, or else into the year-group common rooms, which can be a bit of a noisy nightmare. They've put basketball hoops in the playground now, so you don't have to just play football or just wander around.

The school has fifteen hundred pupils, that's almost three hundred in each year in the lower school, so there's a huge range of people from different backgrounds and with different views on life. This ought to give you a wide choice of friends, but it doesn't work out like that. Usually you just have a little group of four or five people rather like you. Boys and girls keep pretty much separate, and you aren't supposed to hang out with people outside your age group.

A big school like ours is intimidating, and friends are often made because newcomers want someone to hide behind, and to be protected by those who are used to the place. Life can be pretty awful if you don't have a friend, but once you are a year or two into the school almost everyone has found a niche into which they can fit.

Not being with other age groups is supposed to help stop bullying, but it doesn't work, and anyway, you can get bullied by people in your own year group.

Classes don't usually get any bigger than thirty or so, but you get bigger groups for PE and sometimes for drama too, and for trips out. Class sizes seem to get smaller as you go up the school.

At break time I usually go and talk with a few of my friends and just chill on the patio. If you get bored there's plenty of other things to do such as play table-tennis, go on the climbing wall, play on the computer, go to the art room, play a sport, have a big rumble on the mats, read, play music, go out into the town or go and join the people hanging out by the summer house. In the winter me and a few friends will crowd around a radiator and talk, unless it actually snows when we'll go and chuck snowballs at each other or get a teacher to drive us up to the moor.

The school has seventy-odd pupils so you ought to have a small choice of friends, but it doesn't work like that. Usually you have a large group of intimate friends. Boys and girls mix freely and pupils of all ages mix like they have known each other for years. I know everyone and although I don't get on with them all I find it fun to listen in on people's conversations. It's surprising how different each person is. The great thing is that everyone's themselves.

A small school like ours is friendly.

Because everyone is always sort of looking out for everyone else there is hardly any bullying, and people who have been frightened of going to school before often get to feel quite happy and confident here.

Classes don't usually get any bigger than fifteen or so, but you get bigger groups for PE and sometimes for drama too, and for trips out. Class sizes seem to get bigger as you go up the school.

Teachers, lessons and the timetable

The fixed timetable means you are sure to get a balanced education. You can't just concentrate on the subjects you like and ignore all the rest.

The head appoints the new teachers, and I don't see how else it could be done. They're all going to be under his command, so he has to pick people who suit his style. If you asked the student council to take part they'd only choose the softest teachers who would never make them do anything they didn't want to do.

Because the timetable is fixed you do a bit of everything almost every day, and if you're bored in one lesson you have the consolation of knowing that you'll soon be going on to something else.

I'd never have got interested in Biology if I hadn't had to do it, and anyway when you are thirteen you are unlikely to know which specific area you should put all your effort into. Also the subjects complement each other and make the brain work in different ways, so it is good to do them all.

The teachers try to keep their classes all working at the same level, so that they can teach everyone together, but there's always a feeling of competition so the people at the top of the class want to do better, and the people at the bottom of the class have to work really hard to keep up. We are setted for maths and science, and in some other subjects the teachers just have to give different work to different groups or some people will be floundering.

Teachers, lessons and the timetable

The free-choice timetable means you are sure not to waste hours of your time on stuff that simply doesn't interest you or seem to have any relevance to you.

The School Meeting appoints the new teachers and it seems a very good system. Short-listed applicants have to come into the school and actually teach for a day, so we get a really good idea of what they're like as teachers.

Although the timetable is fixed, most people have free periods because of the subjects they aren't doing, and you can carry on doing something that interests you for hours at a time. If you get really genuinely interested you can even miss other lessons, but the teachers get fed up if you miss lessons to go swimming or hang out down in the garden or to build tree-houses.

I'd never have got interested in Biology if it had just been one of the things I had to do. But on the other hand there's a risk that you might not learn to appreciate something because you never had the initiative to try it.

The teachers try to have all their pupils working at their own level, although even then sometimes everyone does the same thing, and in some subjects you can't avoid it. There's no feeling of competition, so people who find it hard don't feel too humiliated. If you don't work the teacher will be able to notice and will enquire what's the matter, partly because they have the time and the closeness. Ultimately the outcome is up to you, anyway.

You have to respect your teachers if you are going to learn anything much from them, so I think it is good that we call them Miss and Sir and that we can't answer back.

We are set an hour or two of homework every evening, which some people think is fair because the teachers put in hours doing preparation and correcting. Some people even claim to enjoy it but I hate it. You can actually get away with doing practically no work or homework right throughout the school. The teachers give up a lot quicker than you might think.

The timetable is king, and it only gets suspended for something really important like a sports day or a large school trip. Even when a teacher is ill you don't get any respite, because either some other teacher takes you, or two classes are put together, or they bring in a supply teacher. Anything rather than let you hang about in the playground.

It's essential to have a set curriculum for everybody to follow, because how can you know whether something is going to interest you until you have tried it?

Our school is always high up in the league tables of exam results. It's because the teachers see to it that we use our time properly and don't waste it socialising.

In lessons you can sit where you like, you call the teachers by their first names and you can ask questions without having to put your hand up first.

In later years you are given homework but most of the time it is optional as it is for your benefit, not for the teachers'.

The timetable is always being changed to let people spend two days working on Macbeth, or for a whole-day science trip somewhere, or to go climbing, or to do special activities with some visitors from abroad, or to rehearse a school play. And when one of the teachers is ill we just have some extra free time, which some people complain about because they prefer having lessons.

It's stupid to have a set curriculum for everybody to follow, because everybody's different, and why should you spend years and years half-heartedly trying to learn a lot of stuff that you are going to forget as soon as the exams are over?

Sands is hardly ever more than about halfway up in the league tables of exam results. It's because there are plenty of us who only came because we weren't doing well at other schools, and some people take the exams early or late, and anyway we don't spend all our time on school subjects here. There's more to life than that.

Mr. H. is a good teacher. He keeps really good discipline so you can get on with your work without being interrupted, and he explains things clearly and helps you when you get stuck. Anyone who isn't attending or who steps out of line in any way gets the rough edge of his tongue, and that really is rough. He's strict but fair, and although most of us are more than a little scared of him, we respect him at the same time. He makes sure we do everything we need to do, so if you're taking exams you know you're going to do as well as you possibly could.

There are some brilliant younger teachers too, who you can really identify with. They keep boundaries but they have a good sense of humour and they really seem to care about your social well-being as well as your academic work.

Mrs. W. is a bad teacher. She can't keep order so it doesn't matter what she gives us to do, because no one does it anyway. She doesn't understand how to control us at all. She shouts and gives us detentions and sends us to the headmaster, but it doesn't make any difference. I want to learn and I hate sitting there seeing her being humiliated. All her lessons are a waste of time.

Rowan *[a compilation of different teachers]* is a good teacher. She always explains things very well and really makes you think, not just write. She loves talking and will answer questions about anything. If one of the pupils says the answer, even if it is wrong she still gets excited. Often we get into quite heated discussions, and it isn't always her side that wins.

She's everyone's friend and she often goes down into the garden with a mug of coffee to chat to students about their problems or just life in general. She will listen to you however personal or complicated your problems are. She should really be employed as a crisis and personal problem-solving person.

She also really tries hard to make the school work and to make people understand it. Just about everybody loves her lessons. She corrects everyone's work really carefully and goes through it with them so they know exactly what they need to do, and if you're taking exams you know she'll help you to do as well as you possibly can.

Brian *[a fiction, like Rowan]* is a bad teacher. Hardly anyone turns up for his lessons, and if you do turn up he gives you such pathetic things to do that you wish you hadn't come. He doesn't understand the school at all but he's always trying to push his opinions on to everyone else. He thinks we should all come to his lessons and sit quietly and listen to him and do just what he says. He is a bit patronising and can be very sarcastic. If people irritate him he gets very angry and grumpy and shouts at them. Most people think he's a complete waste of time.

People who are keen on sport take the PE lessons really seriously. People who are bad at it just hang about out of doors getting cold, or dodge about pitifully in the gym trying to keep out of the way. It keeps them fit, I suppose. It's just the same length as any other lesson, though, so once you have changed into your PE kit there is hardly any time for anything. Out-of-the-way sports like martial arts and skateboarding you have to do outside school in the evenings or at weekends. Two PE sessions a week isn't much, but it means everybody has to take at least some exercise.

What happens outside lessons

Me and my friend used to go into the library at lunchtimes if it was cold weather, but when they started saying we couldn't eat in the lobby and then they stopped letting us play cards, we stopped. I like it in there because I like reading. It is the only place in the school where you can just sit quietly and read; outside it's too noisy. Plus like all libraries it has good fiction books so if you don't like the book you're reading you can get another. I used to take out books regularly but I think I've read all the ones I might be interested in. They need a new collection! There is also a large number of non-fiction which is good if we're doing projects. You can take the book out or take notes at a table. They also have several computers, so if you've forgotten to do your homework, you can quickly do it on one of them, though you usually have to book in advance. Another problem with going in there is that you can get chucked out if you are too noisy. That's not nice when you are all warm and cosy and it's tipping down outside!

People who are keen on sport at Sands play lots of the time but sport at Sands is often played without a teacher or lessons – the pupils often organise the games. The facilities are not as good as at most schools, with only a tennis court for all sports, but people into skateboarding can go to the skatepark if they go in threes. Rock climbing is taken really seriously, and we have a climbing wall in an old building in the grounds. There's a public swimming pool next door to the school, too. And now and again there is a craze for martial arts, or yoga or mountain-biking. Some people never seem to take any exercise at all, though, except maybe walking to school and sometimes swimming.

What happens outside lessons

The English teachers have a good selection of books and there is a wall of books in the little room but we haven't got a library as such. If you are in Meryl's class you can sign out for books when you want to and take them out to read at home. I know one girl who sits reading in Meryl's room just about all day, but most people have too many other things to do. They may start reading a book in the English room and then take it home to finish, but not read it all day at school.

At the end of the day we have to put all the chairs up on the desks to make it easy for the cleaners who come in every evening and sweep round. They can't cope with the chewing gum, but otherwise the place is kept amazingly clean and tidy, and the lino in the corridors is even polished. We don't come to school to learn to do domestic work like that, so it is only reasonable that other people should be paid to do it. Visitors like it, too. It gives a really good impression. But you can volunteer to do cleaning, if you want to, and you get paid for it.

There used to be one music lesson a week for everyone up until Year Ten, but that's stopped now. You can get instrumental lessons for free in school time, though, and there is an orchestra that rehearses on Thursdays after school, and a choir and various groups.

Lessons finish at 4.15. That's what the timetable says, anyway. The timetable also says that Useful Work follows for quarter of an hour. It consists of '15 minutes' at the end of the day when you clean and maintain an assigned area in the school. It was voted in by the School Meeting. So at 4.25 I begin my assigned useful work – collecting the mugs people have left all around the school and washing them up.

Useful Work is organised by the Useful Work Committee whose own Useful Work it is to run around encouraging students to drop what they're doing and switch a hoover on because useful work has priority over everything. This is one of the hardest jobs because sometimes people refuse or shout back at you.

You can help to cook the lunch if you want to, but if you eat school lunches it's compulsory to take your turn with the washing up.

I spend a lot of the day in the music room. I usually go there in break times, I don't use music to stop going to lessons. We have a piano and a drum kit but we don't have a teacher. I think we should have more instruments and maybe someone to come in every week to teach a music lesson. That person would probably get more people to play together more often.

We do have a group of people who play music together but no supervision. The group varies from two people to four. We are all different ages from eleven to sixteen. We do a lot of improvising and making stuff up. Students often teach each other stuff on the piano and drums. Some people bring in their own guitars and amplifiers but we should buy a guitar and a microphone for the school.

One of the things most people hate is having to wear the school uniform. Sometimes it makes little kids feel proud of themselves up to about Year Eight, but after that we nearly all hate it. But the staff seem to think it is one of the most important things in the whole school. People actually get sent home because they are wearing jeans, even if they are only wearing jeans because they haven't got anything else. One of the arguments in favour of uniform is that it stops the people with money from showing off with expensive clothes, but it also sometimes stops the people without money from coming into school at all. And women teachers dangling with earrings and necklaces and bracelets confiscate the girls' jewellery, and if you come in looking really good with just a little bit of mascara and almost invisible lipstick you are sent to the loos to wash it off. And as for nose-studs and dyed hair! They can get you suspended. People cover their rucksacks with drawings and messages from friends and stars and keychains and stickers, all in some last desperate attempt to give themselves some individuality, and not just be another number.

Parents come for parents' evenings to hear how we are doing in our lessons. And some of them come storming up to school to complain, because they think their little darlings are being bullied or they have had something stolen. Usually they never get past the office, but sometimes the Head sees them. But he does always see the parents he wants to complain to, who don't get their children to school on time or see that they do their homework or buy them the proper uniform.

The staffroom and the sixth-form common room are the only places in the school where there are armchairs and newspapers, and people can make themselves tea or coffee and help themselves to biscuits whenever they are free.

People wear what they want at Sands. If we all wore uniforms or had guidelines about what we can and can't wear it wouldn't fit in with the relaxed and individual atmosphere that is such a big part of the school. Some people like to express themselves through fashions and styles and they should be allowed to if that's what they're interested in, e.g. girls sometimes ask teachers to help them make their own clothes or incorporate fashion into their art projects.

When I first came to Sands I got the impression that maybe some of the popular fashion phases going through at that time were the Sands uniform and that everyone dressed in the same style, e.g. the baggy jeans and hoodies everyone wore.

Then I realised that the students create the fashions themselves, so in a way, if it's important to you, you can make up and experiment with your own personal uniform and image.

Parents are quite often to be seen around the school, although some people find their own parents embarrassing and make sure they keep out of the way. They often arrive early at the end of school and come in to speak to some teacher or other, and sometimes there are gardening Saturdays or cleaning or decorating days because we aren't very good at looking after the place ourselves – not up to adult standards, anyway. And there are PTA meetings and parents' evenings to talk about ordinary school work as well.

There isn't a staffroom so in break times the teachers hang around with everyone else, and have just as much difficulty in getting to the kettle as the rest of us do.

Rules and punishments

There are written rules about uniform and attendance and not going out during school hours unless you are in Year Ten or above and not running in the corridors and not climbing the trees in the playground but most of the time behaviour is kept under control by the staff maintaining discipline. They are always around, indoors and out, and if you are out of order they try to deal with it, whether there is a rule about it or not. It's usually only the dinner ladies, who aren't very good at it, and if you disagree with them they send you to the head, and the head can do what he likes with you - even suspend you or actually expel you if he thinks it is justified. But it hardly ever happens.

Two of the most strictly enforced rules are no swearing and no smoking. They're both really bad habits, and although just about everyone swears sometimes when they are out of earshot of the staff, and people smoke in the toilets and when we're waiting for the buses, it's a good thing to try to get it into our heads how bad they are.

Rules and punishments

There are written rules about going out during school hours and doing your share of the washing up and not bringing drugs or alcohol into the school, but the basic ethos is that everybody must have common sense. That means you don't do anything that's stupid if you really think about it. Sometimes someone will do something stupid anyway and it's usually the teachers who calmly disapprove of it. Some students will express their disapproval of perhaps someone dropping litter or breaking something. A very serious incident may be taken by anyone to the School Meeting by writing it up on the public agenda board, and everyone will discuss the consequences. The school meeting can suspend you or even expel you if they think it is justified. But it hardly ever happens.

Nobody minds about swearing, unless it's really offensive, and you used to be allowed to smoke down the garden, away from the main building. Now the rule has been changed to over- sixteen-year-olds being allowed to smoke out of the school grounds, and no one else being allowed to smoke at all. At the moment people who are finding it hard to quit go down the garden and smoke anyway. Because there is no punishment at this moment in time, because we are trying to be trusting about it, the under-age students who do smoke are quite open about it. We are trying to think of something to help people stop smoking altogether.

These are other possible punishments:
    extra work
    detention
    solitary work
    having things confiscated
    taking round a timetable which has to be signed by
    each teacher at the end of a lesson
    being sent to your Head of Year
    being sent to the Head

Some people can't accept authority and are always trying to rebel against it, but they are just nerds who don't understand the system. The school sometimes takes on pupils who have been making a nuisance of themselves in other schools and they take up a lot of staff time. It can be a drag for the rest of us, but usually it works out in the end. Not for everybody, though.

Problems

You can get pot and Es from people in school, but the staff either don't know or pretend they don't know because they wouldn't know what to do about it. They occasionally get people to come in and give lectures about drugs, but nobody takes them very seriously – they only say all that stuff because they have to.

There aren't really any punishments, except for automatic suspension if you bring drugs into school. And if you don't do your share of washing up you can't have school lunches. And if you're a nuisance in a lesson you can be voted out. Sometimes teachers get cross and shout, but there's nothing they can actually do. It doesn't matter because nearly all the time things go smoothly, because the only people in the classrooms are people who have chosen to be there.

The school sometimes has to get rid of pupils who make too much of a nuisance of themselves and take up too much staff time. It makes it better for the rest of us, but they never seem to succeed in getting rid of all of them.

Problems

Drugs get talked about quite a lot, because you can't not come across them if you go out at all in the evenings. The level of the discussion depends entirely on which of the school's easily divisible cliques you focus on. Many of the students have regular experiences with cannabis and this is tolerated and has open discussion. But if ever cannabis is brought to school it is dealt with swiftly and a single offence results in suspension and a second offence mixed with other events can lead to expulsion.

Assembly and RE and school rules and Citizenship classes teach you about right and wrong. If you weren't taught you wouldn't think about them in the right way.

Personal problems are kept out of school. Teachers are not psychiatrists and they mostly stick to what they are good at, which is teaching, although there are always a few who will chat. If things get really bad you can get an appointment to see the school counsellor. Personal things sometimes come up in drama or RE lessons, but they are always general, because if you got on to individual people's real problems it would get really embarrassing.

Some people can't accept authority and are always trying to rebel against it, but they are just nerds who don't understand the system.

Our school has traditions. They are mostly good traditions, and some are fun and tend to bring the school together, but some are outdated, pointless and rigid. We would like to change them but we can't.

Whatever the staff do there always seems to be a hard core of irresponsible people who smoke or sell dope or skive off or bully people or just disrupt their classes. Some of them think of their years at school as a prison sentence, but that just shows what dorks they are.

People talk a lot about questions of what's fair or unfair. When you are always making your own decisions then right and wrong really matter to you.

If people are feeling really down (or really good) it's good to talk to friends and teachers. When you speak to them you are speaking to friends. No one is superior or inferior. It is so much nicer than having a meeting with a counsellor which would make me feel like a freak. Problems are resolved just as well with the teachers because you learn from their experience and no one is embarrassed because they are all completely trustworthy.

People in a democratic school exercising respect etc. don't feel the need to be rebellious and fight against authority — because there isn't one.

Sands has reasons, not traditions. It has an ethos which represents the collected ethics of all those who are part of the school, which means it's ever-changing according to the people who are there.

Everyone knows each other as there are only 70 people in school. There are a few gits but they usually wallow in each other's bad company. And as a member of the anti-bullying committee, I know that bullying is practically non-existent.

What school is for

There are a number of useful things you learn here that aren't on the national curriculum, for instance:
being polite to older people
obedience
making up excuses
how to look tidy and efficient
saying what people in authority want to hear
how to do what you like without getting caught
the importance of not losing face
how to get down to serious work
looking out for yourself and others
fitting in
dealing with your feelings

Anybody is entitled to their individual opinions, but at school you can be very restricted as to how to express them. There are things I don't like about the school, but there's nothing I can do about it so I just accept it and get along as best I can.

You have to work hard at school if you are going to get a decent job, because your exam results make all the difference. The point of going to school is to get qualified. It has nothing to do with your private life.

It's impossible to relax at school. There's really something subconscious about the atmosphere, some latent authoritative force always on your shoulder, that makes you feel the whole time that you are there to be physically doing something – so get to it, etc. Not because you're interested but just because you've got to.

What school is for

There are a number of useful things you learn here that aren't on the national curriculum, for instance:

    being at ease with older people
    co-operation
    not making excuses
    how to look yourself and be comfortable
    expressing your own opinion
    how to do what you like with an easy conscience
    the unimportance of losing face
    when to get down to serious work
    looking out for other people and yourself
    being unique
    showing your feelings

I used to be apathetic about a lot of things, but I guess that responsibility comes with freedom, and now I've found out that I am a person who cares about things, and wants to get things changed.

You have to get a few qualifications for most decent jobs, but you don't need grade As, and you can do some jobs without passing any exams. School isn't about getting good jobs, it's about finding out who you really are.

It's easy to relax at Sands, and just get absorbed in the atmosphere, and then it's difficult to discipline yourself to get down to work, to develop your skills and everything. But I know now that I'm good at English and art and stuff if I could only utilise my skills better.

Schools can't be democracies. You couldn't possibly give an equal vote to the Year Sixes *[10- and 11-year-olds]* and the Sixth Form *[16- to 18-year-olds]*, let alone the staff. It's the staff's job to organise the school and do the teaching, and it's our job to do the learning.

An important thing about school is the hierarchy, and the way the staff can give out rewards and punishments. Without some kind of external incentive there are lots of people who would spend their entire time in school farting about doing nothing.

I would like to say so much about school being so artificial and the actual reality that people are taught not to believe in and the destruction of the individual and the promotion of the one-size-fits-all human beings approach to life and production.

People who come out of state schooling having accepted that the individual is powerless and unimportant have little or no chance of making any real changes to the wider picture. They are likely to accept whatever life throws at them, good or bad, without giving too much thought to actually changing it for the better.

Sands is a democracy. The school is *ideally* really run by everyone who is part of it. Unfortunately I think it's more complicated than this, for instance the biggest voices aren't always the most constructive and thoughtful. A confident person will probably have more influence than someone more introverted who may in fact care more.

An important thing about Sands is how it is 'at one' with the students – on the same level as them. You don't do things that should be your responsibility for sweets, or a reward of some kind – you do it for yourself, not because a higher power instructs you to. Doing things for yourself is what this place is about. I'm writing *this* for myself.

Sands gives you almost complete freedom in how to use the school. Unfortunately a lot of students there do not use all the school's potential, especially those that have enrolled later, from strict, hard-pushing state schools. They can often just be relieved by how they can take advantage of their freedom at Sands, irresponsibly falling under the influence of other dossers.

Sands didn't prepare me for the intensive world of college. It was a big jump, and now I'm dropping courses, because Sands let me choose to learn in my own way, which was quality, not quantity. However, Sands has prepared me for so much – personal relationships, social and philosophical experiences.

Going to school is like going to buy something in a shop. There is all this teaching on offer, and the labs and the sports facilities and the workshops and the library and the music, and even though you are obliged to go there by law, what you do is pick up what you want or what you can, and leave with as many qualifications as possible. It's like pushing a trolley in a supermarket – you don't try to change their way of doing things, you just make use of them.

As Sands really is the combination effect of everyone in it and their in-school behaviour and ethics we need to be sure that newcomers will be compatible to the school's founding ethos. With the collective power to sack and hire staff, change significant rules, even, say, decide when the school's open, you are more than a student, you are a part of the love of the school, its hands and its mind. As long as this stays so, Sands can only lose its magic so much.

Conclusion

These are the aims from the Warnock report, quoted in my introduction: -

> First to enlarge a child's knowledge, experience and imaginative understanding and thus his (or her) awareness of moral values and capacity for enjoyment: and secondly, to enable him (or her) to enter the world after formal education is over as an active participant in society and a responsible contributor to it, capable of achieving as much independence as possible.

The first section of this book consisted of extracts from official publications, so presumably the schools represented accept the views expressed.

The many young people who have contributed to the rest of the book have been able to edit and correct the sections to which they have contributed. Sometimes they have contradicted statements that did not correspond to their own school experience. The resulting picture is complex but accurate.

On the basis of this evidence, how far do the schools that have been described fulfil the aims of the Warnock report?

Which type of school is more likely to help children to enlarge their knowledge?

And at which type of school are they more likely to enlarge their experience?

Where will they exercise a greater awareness of moral values?

What sort of school will help them to increase their capacity for enjoyment?

Whose ex-pupils will be more likely to enter the world as active participants in society and responsible contributors to it?

And who will be most capable of achieving independence?

The answers are not obvious, and the comparisons in this book have raised many other questions that educators need to think about. Should children learn respect for all authority, or is it better for them to learn to be discerning? How do they decide who to respect? Is there a need for a national curriculum, or will children learn more if they are encouraged to follow their own interests? Who should make the school rules, and who should enforce them? Is punishment effective as a way of teaching responsible behaviour? And so on and so on.

A simplistic version of the aim of traditional education is that every child should acquire knowledge. A.S.Neill said he wanted above all that the pupils at Summerhill should be happy. I would like children also to grow up to understand other people's needs, and to be ready to try to meet them. These various aims are not mutually exclusive, but the different approaches described in this book arrange them in different orders of priority.

Almost thirty years after Warnock, two further questions have arisen, which may help to decide their relative merits. Firstly, what kind of school is most likely to reduce the unprecedented level of adolescent mental distress identified by such bodies as Childline and the Samaritans? And, secondly, in a world full of insecurity, prejudice and fear what kind of school will do most to encourage young people to build a secure, tolerant and confident society?